CCSS Genre **Biography**

Essential Question
How can words lead to change?

Nellie Bly
Reporter *for the* Underdog
by Julia Wall

Chapter 1

A Woman in a Man's World

Women **reporters** who write news stories **investigate** all kinds of crimes and injustices today. However, that wasn't always the case.

Nellie Bly became a **journalist**, or reporter, in the late 1800s. Women reporters then usually wrote about gardening and fashion. People believed it was a man's job to report the news. Nellie Bly **shattered** those beliefs.

Nellie Bly became a reporter when she was 21.

WHAT WAS NELLIE BLY'S REAL NAME?

Nellie Bly's real name was Elizabeth Cochran. She was born in Pennsylvania in 1864. Her father died when she was six.

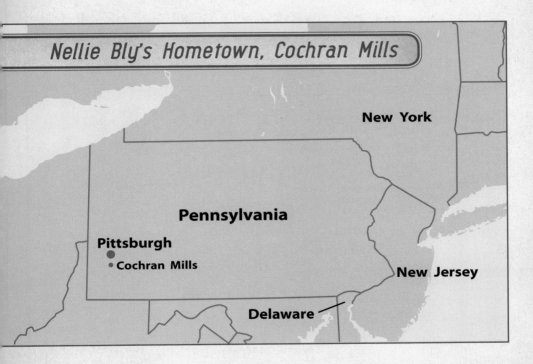

Nellie Bly's Hometown, Cochran Mills

New York

Pennsylvania

Pittsburgh
Cochran Mills

New Jersey

Delaware

The family moved to Pittsburgh when Elizabeth was a teenager. Her mother rented rooms in the house to **boarders** to help pay the bills. Elizabeth wanted to be a teacher, but there wasn't enough money.

HOW COCHRAN BECAME A REPORTER

In 1885, Cochran read a story in a newspaper. It made the **proclamation** that girls didn't need an education or a career. Cochran didn't agree. She wrote to the editor about the story. The editor liked her letter, so he gave her a job!

Most women reporters then did not use their real names. Cochran used the name Nellie Bly. The name was from a **folk** song.

Here is a verse from the folk song "Nelly Bly" by Stephen Foster.

Nelly Bly has a voice
like a turtle dove,

I hear it in the meadow
and I hear it in the grove.

Nelly Bly has a heart warm
as a cup of tea,

And bigger than the sweet
potatoes down in Tennessee.

Women in the 1800s

A woman's job was to take care of her family. People then didn't think women were as smart or as strong as men.

Women did all of the housework. They didn't have washing machines or dishwashers. Cooking, cleaning, and doing laundry took all day.

Women washed clothes by hand in the 1800s.

STOP AND CHECK

How did Nellie Bly get her first job?

Chapter 2

Bly's Daring Jobs

Bly started working as a reporter at the *Pittsburg Dispatch* in 1885. She wrote about things she thought people should know. Her stories often **divided** public opinion. Some people were interested in reading her stories. Other people didn't think they should be written.

Women workers in factories were not paid well.

Bly wrote about poor working conditions in factories. These factories advertised in the newspaper. The money they paid helped produce the newspaper. The factories threatened to stop advertising. Bly's story caused **tension** at the paper. Her editor asked her to choose different topics.

(t and b) Don Bishop/Artville/Getty Images, (tr) Library of Congress Prints and Photographs Division [LC-DIG-nclc-04455]

BLY ON THE RUN

Bly refused to write "safe" stories. In 1886, her editor sent her to Mexico. She wrote about her travels there. She also wrote about a Mexican reporter. He was sent to prison after he complained about Mexico's government.

Bly was almost arrested by the police. She left Mexico. Her stories were published in a book called *Six Months in Mexico*.

Bly moved to New York City and started writing for another newspaper, the *New York World*.

" I was too impatient to work at the usual duties assigned women on newspapers. "

STOP AND CHECK

What kinds of things did Bly write about?

Bly wrote about Blackwell's Island **asylum** in 1887. The asylum was near New York City. Bly pretended to be mentally ill so she could stay there. She ate rotten food and was beaten.

People were shocked when they read Bly's stories. They didn't know the conditions at the asylum were so bad. Then patients were given better care.

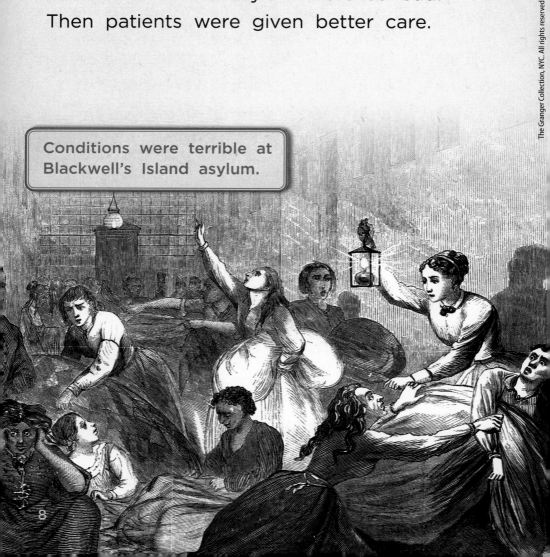

Conditions were terrible at Blackwell's Island asylum.

HELPING ZOO ANIMALS

Bly kept writing stories about injustices. In 1894, she talked to the president of the American Society for the Prevention of Cruelty to Animals. He told Bly the hippo pool at the Central Park Zoo was **filthy**. It needed to be cleaned. The bears had no shelter from bad weather. Bly wrote about the zoo. Then the president showed the zookeepers how to take better care of the animals.

The animals at Central Park Zoo got better shelters.

STOP AND CHECK

How did Nellie Bly help change things in her community?

Chapter 3

Bly Travels the Globe

Bly read the book *Around the World in Eighty Days* by Jules Verne. A character in the book travels around the world in 80 days. Bly decided she would do this.

TRAVELING ALONE

Bly left on November 14, 1889. She went by herself. She traveled in **haste** to complete her trip in 80 days. She wrote stories as she traveled.

Many people **opposed** the idea of women traveling alone. It did not stop Bly.

She traveled to countries like England, France, and Japan. She sent stories about her trip to the newspaper. People enjoyed reading them.

Bly carried a small bag on her journey.

Women and Travel

Women didn't usually travel alone in the 1800s. People thought it was safer for women to travel with others.

Bly returned to New York in only 72 days!

A game called *Round the World with Nellie Bly* was made after Bly's trip.

STOP AND CHECK

Why were people opposed to Bly's journey?

Bly married Robert Seaman in 1895. He owned steel companies. Bly was in charge of one.

Bly took over all the companies when Seaman died in 1904. But the factories closed in 1914 because they owed a lot of money.

World War I began in 1914. Millions of people **perished** during the war. Bly worked as a reporter again. She was the first American woman journalist to report from a war.

Nellie Bly ran the Iron Clad Factories company.

INTO THE DANGER ZONE

Bly reported from the **front line**. She wrote that officers lived in clean conditions. **Regular** soldiers lived in muddy, dangerous trenches.

Bly kept writing after the war. She used her writing and public **addresses** to help her community. She found homes for children and helped women get jobs.

Bly died in 1922 at the age of 57. One newspaper called her "The Best Reporter in America."

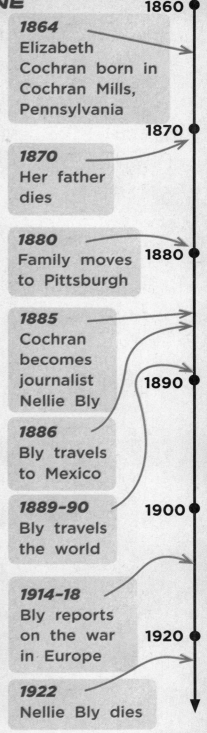

1860

1864
Elizabeth Cochran born in Cochran Mills, Pennsylvania

1870

1870
Her father dies

1880
Family moves to Pittsburgh

1880

1885
Cochran becomes journalist Nellie Bly

1890

1886
Bly travels to Mexico

1889–90
Bly travels the world

1900

1914–18
Bly reports on the war in Europe

1920

1922
Nellie Bly dies

Nellie Bly spoke out for people with no money or power. She wrote about problems and helped to change things.

Bly was brave. Her work took her around the world, but she also helped people at home.

A United States postage stamp **honored** Nellie Bly in 2002.

2002

STOP AND CHECK

What kinds of things did Bly write about during World War I?

Respond to Reading

Summarize

Summarize how Nellie Bly used words to help people. Your graphic organizer may help you.

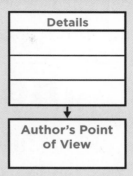

Details

↓

Author's Point of View

Text Evidence

1. What does the author think about Nellie Bly? Use evidence from page 14 in your answer. **AUTHOR'S POINT OF VIEW**

2. Find the word *arrested* on page 7. What does it mean? What clues in the text help you figure it out? **VOCABULARY**

3. Write about why people thought women should not do some things. How did Nellie Bly change their minds? Use details from the text. **WRITE ABOUT READING**

Compare Texts
Read about a trip that helped change people's ideas about women and travel.

Around the World

Nellie Bly got the idea for her journey around the world because she ran out of ideas. Sometimes she found it hard to think up new ones. One week, she thought:

I wish I was at the other end of the earth! (*Around the World in Seventy-Two Days,* page 2)

It gave her an idea. She would try to beat the record set in *Around the World in Eighty Days.* It was hard to plan such a long journey. But Bly had no doubts.

I always have a comfortable feeling that nothing is impossible if one applies a certain amount of energy in the right direction ... (*Around the World in Seventy-Two Days,* page 3)

Bly set off on her journey. She met Jules Verne in Paris. He wrote *Around the World in Eighty Days*. Verne told her that the idea for his book came from a newspaper.

[I] found in it a discussion and some calculations showing that the journey around the world might be done in eighty days. (*Around the World in Seventy-Two Days*, page 22)

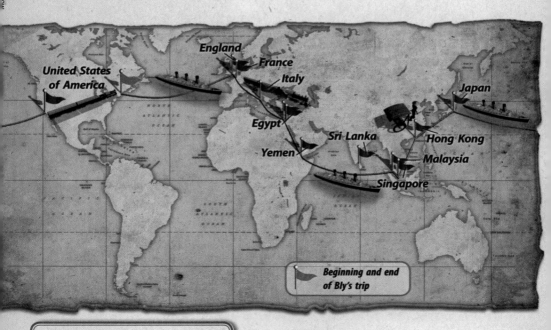

United States of America

England

France

Italy

Egypt

Yemen

Sri Lanka

Japan

Hong Kong

Malaysia

Singapore

Beginning and end of Bly's trip

Bly did her world trip in just 72 days.

Bly knew she had to travel quickly to beat the record.

My only wish and desire [in Hong Kong] was to ... learn the earliest possible time I could leave for Japan, to continue my race against time around the world.
(*Around the World in Seventy-Two Days,* page 74)

Bly still took time to look around her. She wrote about the people and places she saw.

Bly's trip took less than 80 days. She showed that a woman could travel alone in record-breaking time!

Make Connections

How did Nellie Bly's trip change ideas about women's travel? ESSENTIAL QUESTION

What kinds of things did Nellie Bly write about? Why was her trip around the world important?
TEXT TO TEXT

Glossary

asylum *(uh-SIGH-luhm)* a hospital for patients with mental health problems *(page 8)*

boarders *(BOR-durs)* people who stay in a house and pay for a room and meals *(page 3)*

front line *(fruhnt lighn)* the area where an army is close to the enemy *(page 13)*

journalist *(JUR-nuh-list)* a person who writes stories for newspapers or magazines *(page 2)*

Index

Focus on
Social Studies

Purpose To learn about the differences between primary and secondary sources

Procedure

Step 1 ▶ Work with a partner or in a small group. Make a list of the things in this book that came from primary sources.

Step 2 ▶ Talk about the list. How can you tell if information comes from a primary source?

Step 3 ▶ Make a poster that shows the differences between primary and secondary sources. Show how these sources might be useful in your work.